# 50 NIFTY

# SUPER

# Origami Crafts

# 50 NIFTY

# SUPER

# Origami Crafts

Written by Andrea Urton
Additional material by Michelle Ghaffari

Illustrated by James Staunton
Additional illustrations by Neal Yamamoto

## LOWELL HOUSE JUVENILE

### LOS ANGELES

CONTEMPORARY BOOKS

CHICAGO

NOTE: The numbered pinwheel in the upper right-hand corner of each craft indicates the level of difficulty, 1 being the easiest, 3 being the hardest.

Publisher: Jack Artenstein
Director of Publishing Services: Rena Copperman
Executive Managing Editor, Juvenile: Brenda Pope-Ostrow
Editor in Chief, Juvenile: Amy Downing
Director of Art Production: Bret Perry
Cover Crafts: Treesha Runnells
Cover Photograph: Ann Bogart

Lowell House books can be purchased at special discounts when ordered in bulk for premiums and special sales. Contact Department TC at the following address:

Lowell House Juvenile
2020 Avenue of the Stars, Suite 300
Los Angeles, CA 90067

Library of Congress Catalog Card Number: 97-14877

ISBN: 1-56565-730-6

Printed in the United States of America

10 9 8 7 6 5 4 3 2 1

# Contents

# Introduction

The beautiful, sophisticated origami masterpieces made in Japan at least 1,200 years ago were generally made for ceremonies, festivals, or symbolic purposes. It's not known whether Japanese, Chinese, or Korean people first practiced this creative art form, but the word *origami* comes from the Japanese words *ori* (to fold) and *kami* (paper).

Some of the traditional designs for animals, birds, insects, and objects—first created centuries ago—have never changed. So when you build your origami crafts, you are recreating history!

There are as many styles and designs of origami and reasons for making it as there are people who create the pieces. Some people love to come up with new ideas and figure out a way to make their designs work. Others enjoy the challenge of taking a diagram in a book and making it into an even better object than what is pictured.

Regardless of which way you prefer to work, origami is inexpensive and a wonderful form of art you can do practically anywhere.

To bring out the best in every origami craft you create and fold, follow these important tips:

- Always work on a clean, hard surface.

- Neatness is most important when it comes to making origami figures. Until you become familiar with the various folds, practice your folding techniques on scratch pieces of paper, trimmed to make all four sides equal.

- Crease firmly and precisely, making each fold even and crisp. The sharper your creases, the better your finished piece will look.

- Never skip a step.

- The best way to become really good at doing anything—especially origami—is to practice, practice, practice. Then, practice some more!

Now you're ready to learn and perfect one of the most beautiful and original art forms around. You'll learn basic folds and forms that are used throughout all 50 origami projects. Then you'll discover fun ways to show off your art as centerpieces, room decorations, and much more!

# Getting Started with Origami

To some people this may look like nothing more than a stack of paper. To those who can perform the ancient oriental art of origami, this stack can be a barnyard full of animals, a fleet of boats sailing on a paper ocean, or even a spacecraft rocketing through a field of paper stars. No matter what you choose to make, origami is an adventure. Let's begin by looking at the basics.

## Basic Materials

A few of the designs in this book require the use of scissors, but generally the only material you will need is paper. Any thin, square paper will do, but special origami paper is available at art supply and specialty stores. It is colored on one side, white on the other, and precut into squares. Once the form is complete, you can sketch on details or use glitter, feathers, cotton wool, or other materials to make your creation unique. Let your imagination go!

## Basic Folds

The figures in this book are accompanied by written instructions and diagrams to help you through each step. Simply follow the direction of the arrow when making your fold. There are two basic folds that you will need to know:

### The Valley Fold

Fold the paper toward you.
In the diagrams, a valley fold
is represented by a line
like this: – – – – – – –

### The Peak or Mountain Fold

Fold the paper away from you.
In the diagrams, a peak or mountain
fold is represented by a line
like this: –·–·–·–·–·–

### IMPORTANT TIP!

When making your origami figures, remember that neatness counts! *Always* work on a smooth, hard surface and make each crease as even and crisp as possible. Sharp creases make the form easier to work with and they make your finished project look better. If you make a mistake, start over with a fresh piece of paper.

## Basic Forms

The following forms are the basis for many different figures. They are listed here in order of difficulty, from beginner to advanced. Take some time to practice and get used to these forms. Some are more challenging than others, but once you master the basics, you will be ready to create the 50 nifty figures in this book or even design some of your own. The 50 nifty origami crafts begin on page 18. Happy folding!

## Basic Form 1

1. Begin with a square piece of
   paper in a flat diamond shape.
   Note that in the diagram the
   corners are labeled A and B.
   Fold your paper in half as
   shown, bringing point A to meet
   point B.  Make a sharp crease
   across the fold, then reopen it
   into a square.

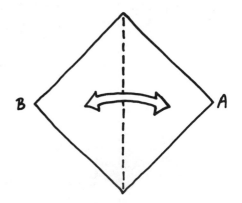

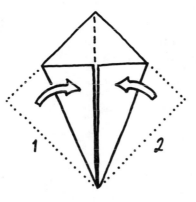

2. Now fold sides 1 and 2 to the
   center line.  Your paper should
   look like a kite.

## Basic Form 2

1. Begin with a square piece of
   paper in a flat diamond shape.
   Fold your paper in half as
   shown, bringing point A to
   meet point B, and make a
   sharp crease.

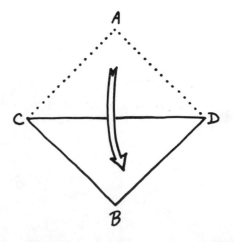

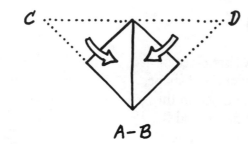

2. Now fold points C and D to meet points A-B and the form is complete.

## Basic Form 3

1. Begin with a square piece of paper. Fold the paper in half from side to side, then top to bottom to form the creases shown. Then reopen it into a square.

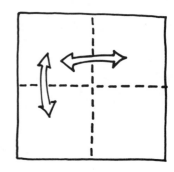

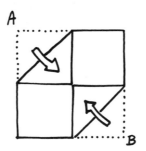

2. Next, fold points A and B to the center.

3. Finally, fold points C and D to the center.

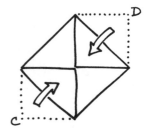

## Basic Form 4

1. First, complete the instructions for Basic Form 1, then fold points C and D (at the wide end of the kite) to the center line and make two sharp creases. Now fold the form in half, bringing point E to meet point F.

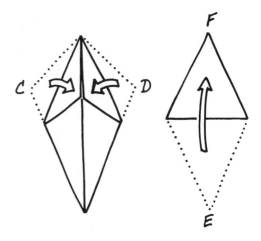

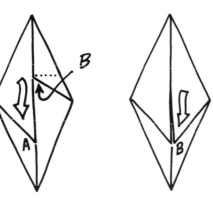

2. Carefully open the form back to a kite. Then, while holding down point B with your fingertip, lift point A up and fold it toward the center line. Repeat the same fold with point B.

## Basic Form 5

1. Begin with a square piece of paper. Fold your paper in half from side to side. Next, open the paper to a square, then fold it from top to bottom. Reopen the paper and fold it diagonally both ways. Now when you reopen the paper to a square you should have the pattern of creases shown in the illustration.

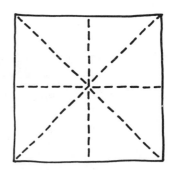

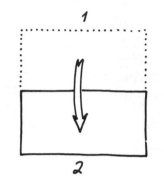

2. Fold down side 1 to meet side 2.

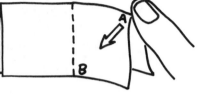

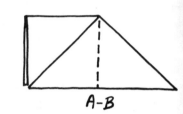

3. Hold the right side of the form open at point A, then push down on it to meet point B, making a flat triangle.

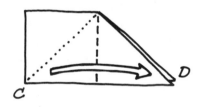

4. Fold point C to meet point D.

5. Repeat steps 3 and 4 with the left side and your form is ready.

## Basic Form 6

1. Begin with step 1 of Basic Form 5.

2. Turn the paper to form a diamond shape, then fold point A to meet point B.

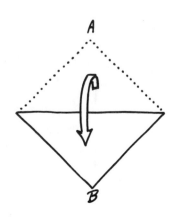

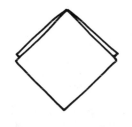

3. Carefully hold the right side of the form open at point C, then push down on it to meet point D, making a flat diamond shape.

4. Fold point E to meet point F.

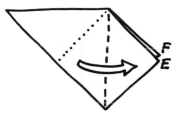

5. Repeat steps 3 and 4 with the left side of the form.

## Basic Form 7

1. To make this form you must first follow all of the steps in Basic Form 6.

2. Using only the top layer of paper, fold points A and B to the center line, then fold down point C. Remember to make those creases sharp and crisp!

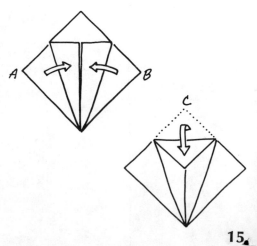

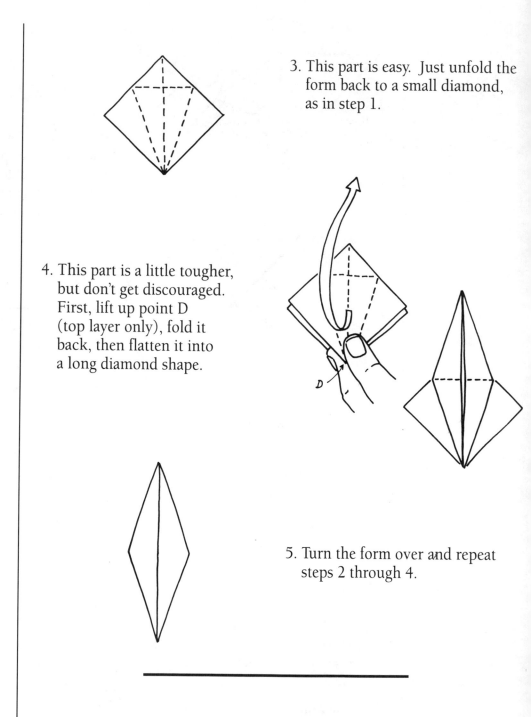

3. This part is easy. Just unfold the form back to a small diamond, as in step 1.

4. This part is a little tougher, but don't get discouraged. First, lift up point D (top layer only), fold it back, then flatten it into a long diamond shape.

D

5. Turn the form over and repeat steps 2 through 4.

## Basic Form 8

1. Begin this form with step 1 of Basic Form 5, then fold sides 1 and 2 toward the center line.

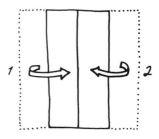

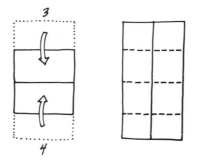

2. Now fold sides 3 and 4 up to the center line. Make a nice, sharp crease, then unfold it.

3. Next, you must make two diagonal creases across the center. Do this by first folding point A to meet point B. Crease the paper sharply, then unfold it. Now repeat this step on the opposite side, bringing point C to meet point D.

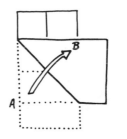

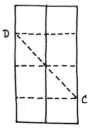

4. This step might take some practice. Lift points E and F up and out, then flatten the form. Repeat this step with points G and H and this tricky form is finished.

# This Little Piggy

Here's a fine, plump pig to begin a barnyard scene. It's complete with a flat pig snout. Going one step further will give your pig a curly tail to wiggle, too.

**Directions**

1. Begin with a square and fold sides 1 and 2 to the center, then turn the form over and fold sides 3 and 4 to the center.

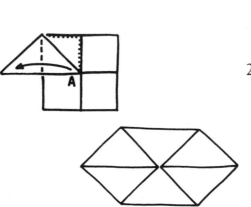

2. Next, pull out point A on the upper left square as shown, and flatten it into a triangle. Now repeat this step with each of the squares.

3. Using a mountain fold, turn back point B. Use a valley fold to bring points C and D to point E, then fold back points F and G.

4. It won't be long now before your plump little porker takes shape. Use a mountain fold to fold the form in half with the opening at the top.

5. With the longer side of the form facing down, you're ready to make the legs by folding point H (front flap only) forward and point I (front flap only) back as shown.

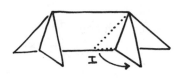

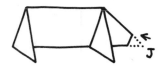

6. Now fold point I down, then repeat steps 5 and 6 on the back of the form.

7. There's only one more thing to do: Tuck in point J to make the pig's flat snout.

## One Step Further

**What You'll Need:**
glue • marking pen • curling ribbon

Draw eyes and a mouth on your pig. Make its curly tail by gluing on about an inch of curling ribbon.

**19**

# Down on the Farm

With its peaked roof and wide door, this barn sets the scene for all of the origami chickens and pigs you'll create.

**Directions**

1. Begin with Basic Form 5, then fold point A and point C up to meet point B. Turn the form over and repeat this step with the remaining layer.

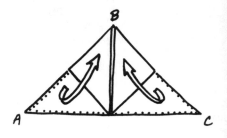

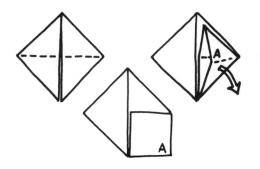

2. You now have a diamond shape. Fold this in half to make a crease and unfold, then lift up the triangle on the right side and push on point A to form a square.

3. Lift up the triangle on the left side and push on point C to form a square. Then turn the form over and repeat steps 3 and 4 on the other side.

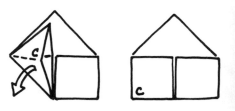

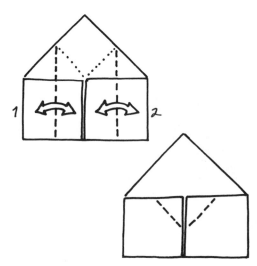

4. Fold outside edges 1 and 2 to the center to make a crease, then unfold them again. Follow this by folding and unfolding triangle shapes on each "door" to make creases as shown.

5. To create the large front door, fold point A to meet point D, and point C to meet point E.

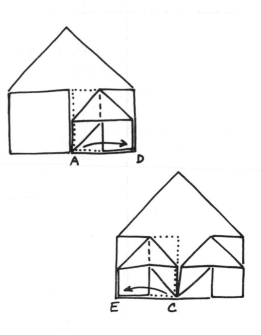

6. To finish, fold up the center triangle.

# One Step Further

**What You'll Need:**
shoebox lid ● sand ● Popsicle® sticks ● mirror

To create a mini-barnyard, stand your barn in the center of a shoebox lid. Popsicle sticks glued to the inside edge of the lid make a perfect fence. Fill the lid with sand for your paper pigs to root in. You can even lay a small mirror in the box to serve as a tiny pond for birds to bathe in!

# Super Simple Sailboat

You'll sail right through folding this little boat and in no time launch it across a tabletop sea.

**Directions**

1. Begin with Basic Form 1 and fold points A and B back to meet sides 1 and 2.

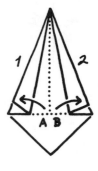

2. Use a valley fold to fold the form in half and create your sail.

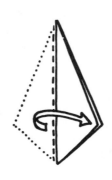

3. To make the base of the boat, fold up point C in a valley fold, crease, and unfold. Then turn up point C to form a "pocket" around point D.

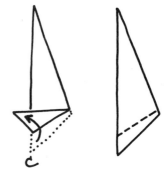

4. To make your boat "seaworthy," fold back point E as shown and set your sails!

# Hatful of Fun

By using paper of different sizes, you can make a hat to fit anyone. Use gift-wrapping paper to make a hat for any occasion!

## Directions

1. Begin with Basic Form 2 and fold up the front flaps only of points A and B, then fold points A and B back as shown.

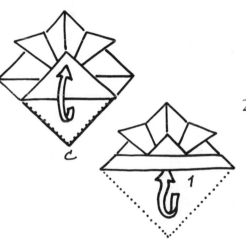

2. Now fold the front flap only of point C in the direction of the arrow, then fold up side 1.

3. Tuck in the back flap, and your hat is ready to wear.

## One Step Further

**What You'll Need:**
glue • glitter • confetti

Make a fashion statement! Decorate the finished hat by gluing on glitter or confetti.

# Toadless Toadstool

Whether you call it a toadstool or a mushroom, if you use your imagination you can picture a tiny elf perched under this origami creation.

**Directions**

1. Begin with Basic Form 3 and unfold the bottom triangle. Use a valley fold to fold down side 1, then turn the form over.

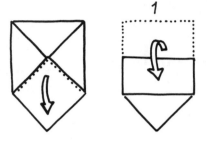

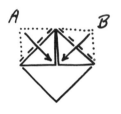

2. The cap of your toadstool is easy to make. Simply fold points A and B in valley folds to the center line.

3. Now reach inside the triangle on the upper right and fold the inside flap only to the center line. Repeat this step with the triangle on the upper left side of the form.

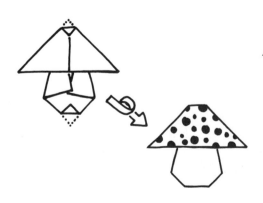

4. Here's the last step. Make small valley folds at the top and bottom of the form and turn it over to see the finished toadstool. Add different-sized dots to your toadstool for a spotty look!

# Angelic Origami

How can paper be angelic?  You'll see when you fold this lovely origami angel, which can stand in a window or on a mantel as a perfect holiday decoration.

## Directions

1. Begin with Basic Form 2, with the opening in the back.  Then fold points A and B to the center line.

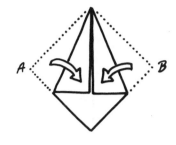

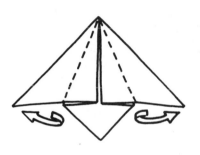

2. Next, unfold the back flaps. These will soon be the angel's wings.

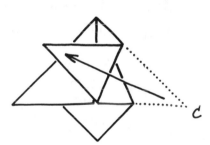

3. Now fold point C over to the left and crease it well, then fold it back to the right as shown.

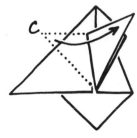

4. You now have a little flap across the center line.  This is point D. Use a valley fold to fold it in the same direction as point C.

**25**

5. Repeat steps 3 and 4 on the left side of the form, then turn the form over.

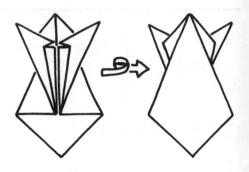

6. To give your angel heavenly detail, fold in points E and F as shown. Use a mountain fold to turn back point G. This flap will allow your angel to stand.

## One Step Further

**What You'll Need:**
glue • glitter • cotton ball • pipe cleaner

Make your angel sparkle by gluing glitter to the wings. Then spread cotton at the base so that your angel appears to be standing on a fluffy cloud. Finally, bend a pipe cleaner into a small circle at one end. Glue the straight end to the back of your angel and presto, she's got a halo!

# A Tisket, a Tasket

Your friends will love this special bird basket!

**Directions**

1. Begin with Basic Form 1 and fold points A and B to the center.

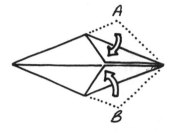

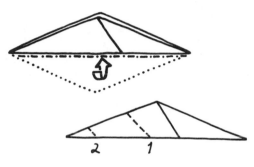

2. Now use a mountain fold to fold the form in half with the opening at the top, then fold and unfold the paper to make two creases as shown.

3. Tuck in fold 1 to create the bird's long neck.

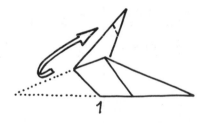

4. Finally, tuck in fold 2 to form its slender beak.

**One Step Further**

**What You'll Need:**
marking pen • name tags • party candy

During a party, this lovely bird basket can be perched at each guest's place setting. Tuck a name tag into the fold at the bird's back or, for a special treat, fill the basket with candy.

# The Great Frame Fold-Up!

Here's the perfect way to show off your favorite photos.

**Directions**

1. Begin with Basic Form 3 with the open side down. Fold all four corners to the center, then turn the form over and repeat this step.

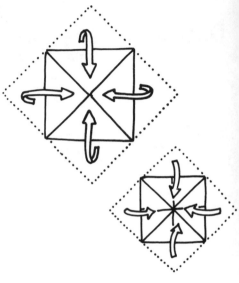

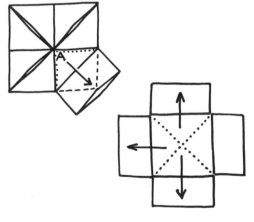

2. Now turn the form over again and lift point A up and out to form a square, as shown in the illustration. Repeat this step at each corner, then turn the form over once again.

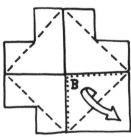

3. Unfold point B (top flap only) from the center as shown, then repeat this step at each corner, then . . . you guessed it! Turn the form over.

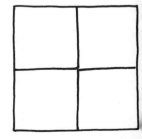

4. The final step is to slip your snapshot into the square at the center of your new paper frame!

# One Step Further

**What You'll Need:**
cardboard • scissors • glue

Make your creation stand by cutting a piece of cardboard the same size as your frame. Cut a two-inch-wide strip of cardboard that is half that length. Finally, glue the strip to the center of the cardboard square for support and glue your frame to the front of the square.

# Cozy Cottage

There's no place like home, and no easier way to build your cozy cottage than with these few steps.

**Directions**

1. Begin with a square and fold sides 1 and 2 to the center.

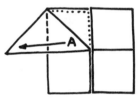

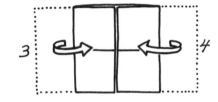

2. Next, turn the form over and fold sides 3 and 4 to the center.

3. To build the roof, pull out point A on the upper left square as shown in the illustration, then flatten it into a triangle.

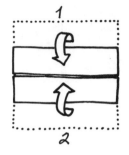

4. Repeat step 3 with the upper right square, turn the form over, and you're almost ready to move in!

**One Step Further**

**What You'll Need:**
marking pen • cotton ball • green food coloring • glue

Complete your home by drawing a door and windows. You can do a little landscaping, too. Start by adding one or two drops of green food coloring to a cup of water. Lightly dip a small cotton ball into the water, allow the ball to dry, then glue it near the door of your house to create a tiny green bush!

#
# Perfect Pinwheel

This pinwheel can be lots of fun on a windy day.

**Directions**

1. Begin with Basic Form 8.

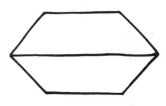

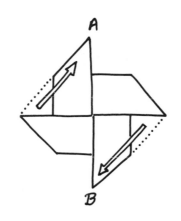

2. Fold point A up and B down as shown and you have a pinwheel. Wasn't that easy?

**One Step Further**

**What You'll Need:**
tack ● two Popsicle® sticks ● glue

To make your pinwheel work, glue the two Popsicle sticks together to serve as a handle. Now stick a small tack through the center of the pinwheel and secure it lightly to the handle. Use a double pinwheel to dress up the design. Now wait for the wind or just blow, blow, blow!

# A "Neat" Neat Coaster

Have you ever picked up a glass to find that it has left behind a wet ring on your table? Since neatness counts, follow these simple directions and turn two small squares of paper into a really neat coaster.

## Directions

1. Begin with paper in a diamond shape, fold it in half, then fold point A (front flap only) to meet point B. Complete this step by turning the form over and repeating the fold on the other side.

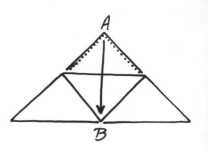

2. Using a mountain fold, fold back point C, while using a valley fold to fold point D forward. You now have form 1. Repeat steps 1 and 2 to make form 2.

3. Follow the illustration and slip the tip of form 1 into the pocket of form 2 and the tip of form 2 into the pocket of form 1 . . . and there you are!

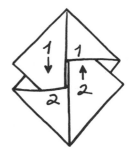

## One Step Further

**What You'll Need:**
gift-wrapping paper • scissors

You can decorate a party table with these coasters. Make place mats by using large sheets cut from wrapping paper.

# Creative Candle Cradle

Can a piece of paper be strong enough to support a candle? It can if you fold it the origami way! For a festive candleholder, make this form with foil-backed origami paper from the art- or craft-supply store. On page 31 you'll find directions for folding an origami candle to complete the mood.

**Directions**

1. Begin with Basic Form 3 with the open side down, and fold points A, B, C, and D to the center.

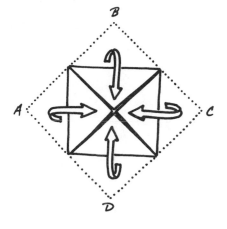

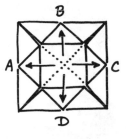

2. Carefully fold points A, B, C, and D back to meet the outside edges of the form.

3. So far so good? Then on to the next step. Using a mountain fold, fold the form in half, then push points A and C toward the center and tuck them in as shown.

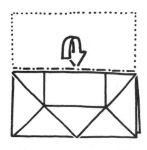

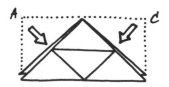

4. Be sure your form is nice and flat, then fold and unfold the top to make a sharp crease.

5. Open the form loosely and push the middle of the "star" down and in to form a four-pointed "bowl" in the center.

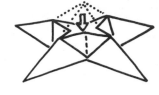

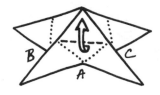

6. Finally, unfold points A, B, C, and D.

# A Clever Candle

Here's a candle that is always lit but never melts. It is the perfect match for the origami candle holder on page 33.

**Directions**

1. Begin with paper in a square. First, fold points A and B to the center line, then use mountain folds to fold back sides 1 and 2 to the center line.

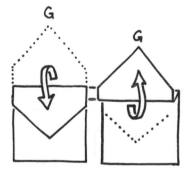

2. Fold points C and D to meet E and F, then use a valley fold to fold up side 3 about one quarter of an inch.

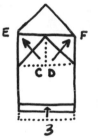

3. Turn the form over and fold point G down, then fold point G up again part way as shown in the illustration.

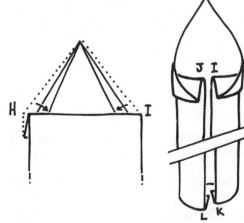

4. Turn the form over once more. Fold down points H and I, then "round out" your candle by bringing the sides together and inserting point I into point J, and K into L.

5. You won't need a match to light this candle. Just twist the pointed tip of the paper to form the flame.

# Wrap It Up

Here's a way to make a small gift even more special—present it in a box that you created yourself.

**Directions**

1. Begin with your paper in a square. Fold the top and bottom of the paper to the center, then fold all four corners in as shown.

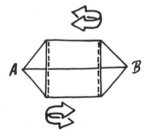

2. Find points A and B. Fold them both toward the center, make a nice sharp crease, and unfold them again.

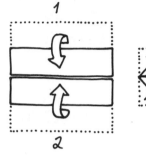

3. Ready for the next step? Open the upper left corner to form a square, then pull point C up and across as shown. Repeat this step with the other three corners. Finally, use mountain folds to fold back sides 1 and 2, crease, then unfold.

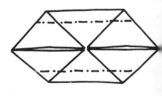

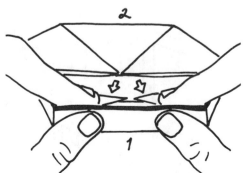

4. Here's where you have to pay close attention! Put your index fingers above the crease (heavy line) on side 1 and your thumbs below the crease. Use the illustration as a guide. Firmly pinch the paper together. This will form one side of your box.

5. By repeating step 4 on side 2, sides 3 and 4 will naturally be drawn up. Simply tuck them into place and your box is almost ready.

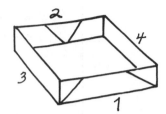

6. Make a top for your box by using a slightly larger piece of paper and following steps 1 through 5.

# A Real Clucker

A farm scene would not be complete without a chubby hen in the barnyard. If you use one large piece of origami paper and several smaller ones, you can create a whole family of chickens!

**Directions**

1. Begin the mother hen with Basic Form 1, then turn the paper over and fold point A to meet point B.

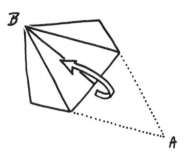

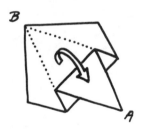

2. Now fold point A back again. About half of the triangle should overlap past the edge of the paper.

3. Next, turn the form over and fold point B to meet point C. Once that step is complete, fold point A toward point C (it will not quite reach point C).

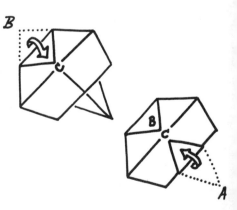

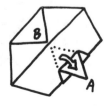

4. To make the hen's sharp beak, fold point A back again about two-thirds of the way, so the points overlap the edge.

5. The body will begin to take shape when you use a valley fold to bring point D to meet point E.

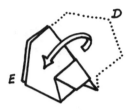

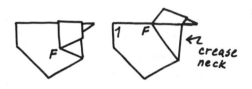

6. Pull up on the hen's head until point F is even with line 1, then crease the neck as shown in the illustration.

7. Finally pull the beak down into position. Repeat the above steps using smaller pieces of paper to create the mother hen's baby chicks.

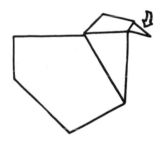

## One Step Further

**What You'll Need:**
glue • feathers • pencil

With a little imagination, you can really bring your chicken family to life. Glue feathers on the tails, wings, and wherever else you want. Draw eyes on each little critter.

# A Whale of an Idea

By using a large square of gift-wrapping paper, you can make a really big whale. Then go one step further so you can yell, "Thar she blows!"

**Directions**

1. Begin with Basic Form 4. Turn the form over so that the opening is on the back. Fold points A, B, and C toward the center line.

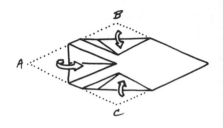

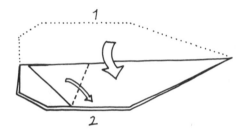

2. Fold the paper down so that lines 1 and 2 meet, then fold back the whale's fins.

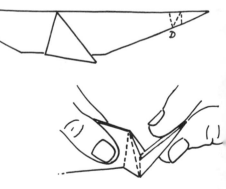

3. Now make the creases as shown near point D. While holding the tail just below the first crease, spread the tip open and up.

**One Step Further**

**What You'll Need:**
cotton ball • paper clip

You can make your whale appear to be spouting. Tear a small amount of material from the cotton ball and spread it out. Twist the bottom half to form a stem. Paper-clip the stem into the opening in the paper above the whale's head.

# Chattering Bird

With your help, this bird will flap its wings and open and close its beak. You can almost hear it chattering.

**Directions**

1. Begin with Basic Form 4 and fold point A to meet point B. This will make a triangle with two smaller triangles inside.

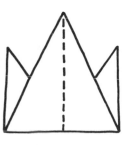

2. Gently grasp the tips of each of the smaller triangles and pull them out to the sides. Once you have a shape that looks something like a crown, fold and unfold the form, creasing it as shown.

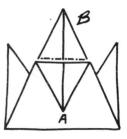

3. To give the bird a beak, simply fold point A toward you and point B away from you. Crease the paper sharply, then unfold point B.

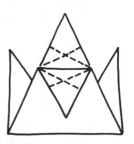

4. Fold and unfold both halves of the beak to make the creases shown in the illustration.

5. Finally, fold the wings away from you until they meet. As you do this the beak will start to close. Pull carefully on the ends of the beak until the form is flat.

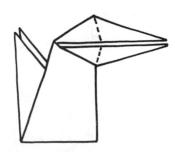

# Precious Pup/Cuddly Kitty

This form is actually two-faced! Fold your paper into a floppy-eared puppy, or turn it over, make a few different folds, and presto—you've created a cat! You'll need a pen to draw in your new pets' faces.

**Directions**

1. First, form a triangle with the fold at the top by folding the paper in half and bringing point A to meet point B.

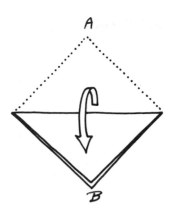

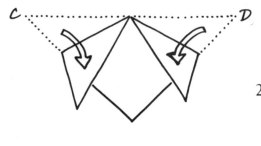

2. To form the puppy's floppy ears, fold points C and D down, then fold points A-B and point E back and the pup's head will take shape. Finish your puppy by drawing eyes, a nose, and a little mouth.

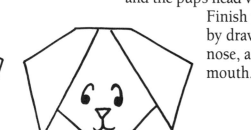

**One Step Further**

You can use this design to make a cuddly kitty by following steps 1 and 2. Then turn the form over and around so that the ears point up. Now fold back points A-B and your kitty is ready for eyes, nose, and a mouth—and don't forget the whiskers.

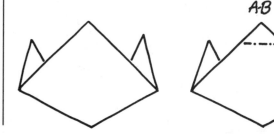

# Paper Pest

This little fly won't bother anyone—it doesn't buzz around, and it will never land where it isn't invited.

## Directions

1. Begin with Basic Form 2 (with the open points at the top). Fold points A and B about halfway down to make the fly's wings.

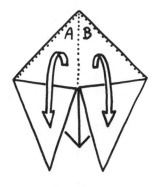

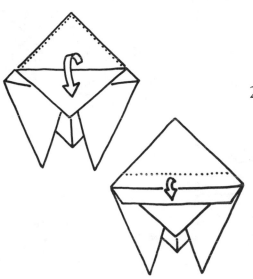

2. Now there are two triangular flaps pointing up. Fold only the front flap down not quite halfway to form a triangle, then fold the base of this triangle down, even with the wings.

3. Is your fly starting to bug you yet? Give it shape by using mountain folds to turn the sides under.

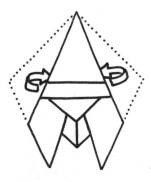

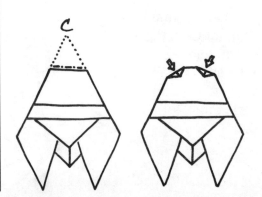

4. To complete the paper pest, form the head by folding point C under, then fold both corners back to give your fly real bug eyes.

43

# Flashy Fighter Jet

You won't need a model airplane kit to turn an ordinary piece of paper into "fly" paper.

**Directions**

1. To prepare for take-off, form a triangle by folding point A to meet point B, then fold point A back again about two-thirds of the way up.

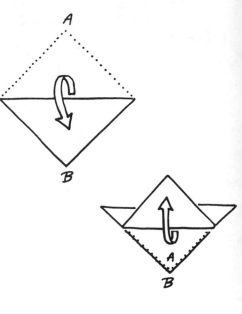

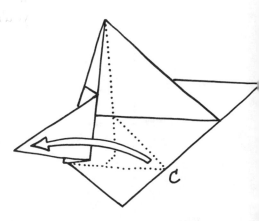

2. You'll need to concentrate here. Use the illustration as a guide and fold the left corner over so that point C touches line 2, then fold the left side over to meet the midline crease.

3. Are you ready to manufacture the wings? Lift point C on the left side of the form, move it gently back to the left and lay it flat, then repeat steps 2 and 3 on the right side of the form.

4. To make the needle nose of the plane, fold point A down in a valley fold, then back in a mountain fold as shown.

5. You're almost ready to start your engines! Using a valley fold, fold the model in half.

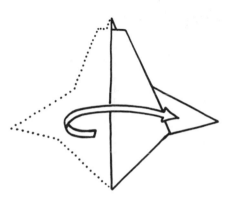

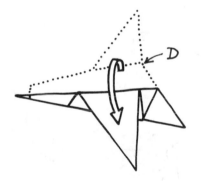

6. Fold down one wing so that point D meets the bottom fold.

7. Turn the form over and repeat step 6. Now spread out the wings and you're ready to soar!

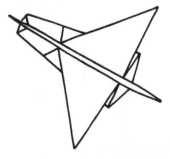

# Cute Cup

This paper cup is very simple to make, but it can come in handy to hold candy, pebbles, paper clips, and maybe even a few sips of water. But drink fast!

## Directions

1. Begin the form with a triangle (fold at the bottom) by folding the paper in half and bringing point A to meet point B.

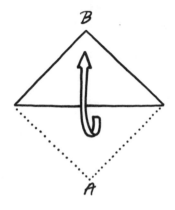

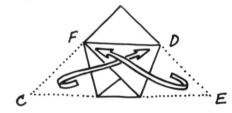

2. Fold point C to meet point D, and point E to meet point F.

3. There's not much more to do—simply tuck the front upper flap into the front triangle, then tuck the back upper flap into the cup.

## One Step Further

**What You'll Need:**
string • sharp pencil or scissors

Turn your cup into a tiny purse or baby bucket! Just poke a hole in both sides of the cup with a sharp pencil or the tip of your scissors. Now pull string through each hole and make a knot on each end, and you'll have a handle to carry your load!

# Handy Holder

Things are easier to find if you have a special place to put them. Here is a design for a handy holder that will keep all of your pencils, marbles, or precious keepsakes within easy reach.

## Directions

1. Begin with Basic Form 5, open end up, then fold over point A (front flap only).

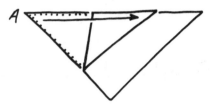

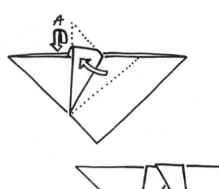

2. Now fold point A back and tuck the tip inside the top of the form. Repeat steps 1 and 2 with the left side of the form, then turn the form over and repeat steps 1 and 2 with both sides.

3. Here's the final step. Fold point B up and back to make a sharp crease. Gently slip your finger inside and open the holder while flattening the base at point B.

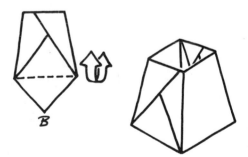

## One Step Further

**What You'll Need:**
scissors • cardboard

To make your handy holder strong, cut a square of cardboard that is slightly smaller than the base. Slip the square inside and to the bottom of the form to act as a support. Now put your treasures inside!

# Hot-Air Balloon

You won't need a string to keep your paper balloon in place, but you will have to blow it up.

**Directions**

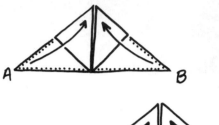

1. Begin with Basic Form 5 and fold points A and B (front flaps only) to the center, then turn the form over and repeat step 1.

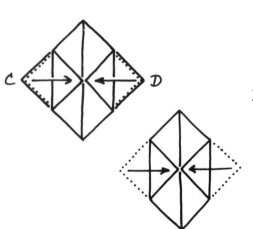

2. Now fold points C and D to the center, turn the form over again, and repeat step 2 on the other side.

3. Fold and unfold points E and F (front flaps only) to make a sharp crease.

4. Next, tuck points E and F into the center triangles as shown, then turn your form over and repeat step 3 on the other side.

5. Finally, blow into the hole at the bottom of the form and your balloon will inflate before your eyes.

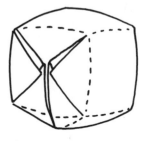

# The Flying Crane

A traditional origami form, the flying crane is challenging to fold, but it's worth the effort.

**Directions**

1. Begin with Basic Form 7, with the two open points facing down.

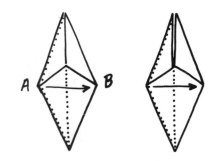

2. Fold point A (front flap only) to meet point B. Turn the form over and repeat this step.

3. Now fold up point C (front flap only), then turn the form over and repeat this step.

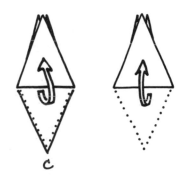

4. Reach inside, pull out the two inner points, flatten the form, and it will look like a three-pointed crown.

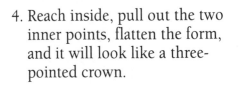

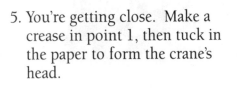

5. You're getting close. Make a crease in point 1, then tuck in the paper to form the crane's head.

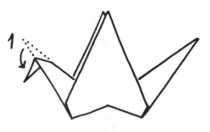

6. The last step is to make the wings curve slightly. Roll each wing around a pencil, then unroll them, and your crane is ready for flight.

## One Step Further

In one hand, hold your crane at its base. With your other hand, move the tail toward the head, then back again. The crane will flap its wide wings.

# The Star Attraction

You'll shine when you show your friends this four-pointed star. It's fun to make and is a perfect decoration for holiday packages.

**Directions**

1. Begin with Basic Form 7 with the two open points up. Fold point A (front flap only) up to meet points B and C.

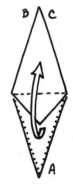

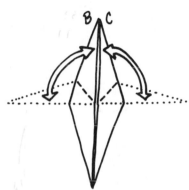

2. Then turn the form over and fold and unfold points B and C to make creases as shown.

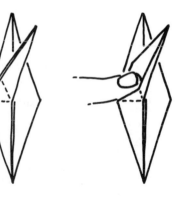

3. Now lift the left triangle until it is at a right angle to the form. Slip your finger into the opening on the side of the raised triangle. Open it slightly.

4. On the center of the star, push down and out to flatten the left triangle. Repeat this step on the right side of the form and your heavenly star is finished.

# Friendship Ring

With one piece of paper you can make a matching pair of rings—one for you and one for a friend.

**Directions**

1. Begin by sharply creasing your paper in the center and tearing it into two equal pieces. You will be using one half-sheet for each ring you make.

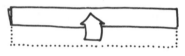

2. Now hold one of the halves of paper lengthwise, fold the outer edges into the center, then fold the paper once more to make a long, thin strip.

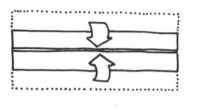

3. At one end of the strip, fold and unfold point A, then fold down side 1 to form a square so that point A meets point B.

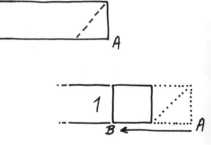

4. Fold over one more time, unfold to a long strip again, then use a mountain fold to turn point C back to meet point D as shown.

5. Use a mountain fold again to fold point E back to meet point F. You will find that you have formed a thick triangle at the back of your ring and your paper should look like an L on its side.

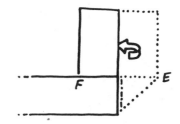

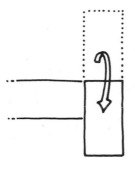

6. Now use a valley fold to fold the upper leg of the L down.

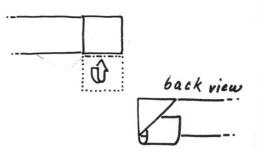

back view

7. Tuck the lower square behind the form and into the triangle at the back of the ring.

8. Finally, fold back the corners at the long end of the strip, curl it around, and tuck it into the open end of the square. If your ring is too large, cut some length off of the long end of the strip before you tuck it in. Now use the other half of your paper to make a matching ring for your special friend.

# Fluttering Butterfly

Use several sheets of paper of different colors to make a bevy of beautiful butterflies.

## Directions

1. Begin with Basic Form 8 and use a mountain fold to fold the form in half, open side up.

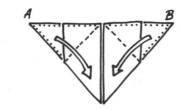

2. Fold points A and B down as shown.

3. Finally, turn the form over, then fold it in half and unfold it to make a sharp crease between the butterfly's wings. Turn out points C and D to give the back of each wing more shape.

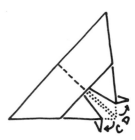

## One Step Further

**What You'll Need:**
pipe cleaners • glue

Glue pipe cleaners to your butterfly to serve as its body and antennae.

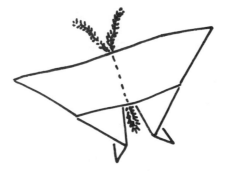

# A Real Turtleneck

It may not cross the finish line in any races, but this turtle will still be a winner with one sheet of paper, a pair of scissors, and your creativity.

**Directions**

1. Begin with Basic Form 2 and fold points A and B (front flaps only) up to meet point C.

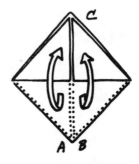

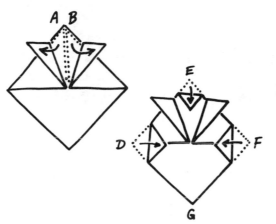

2. Fold A and B down as shown, then fold down points D, E, and F.

3. Are your scissors on hand? Fold point E up again about halfway. Next, make a small cut in the center (front flap only) above point G.

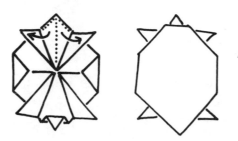

4. Finally, fold out the two flaps made by cutting the paper. Turn the form over and your turtle is complete.

**One Step Further**

**What You'll Need:**
glitter • sequins • glue • safety pin

Decorate your turtle's shell with glitter or sequins. You can wear your creation as a pin by gluing a safety pin to the back side!

# A Terrific Teddy

Once you've followed these few simple steps, you'll have a little critter cute enough to give a big bear hug, especially if you glue on tiny button eyes!

**Directions**

1. Begin with Basic Form 2 and fold up points A and B (front flaps only) to meet point C.

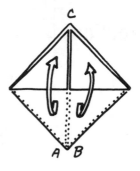

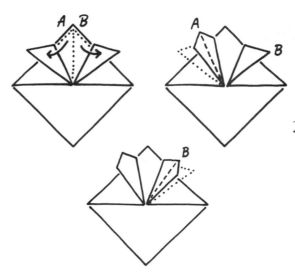

2. Now fold A and B down as shown, then lift point A up at a right angle to the form and press down to flatten it. Repeat this step with point B.

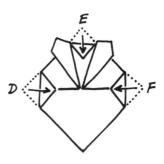

3. Fold down points D, E, and F, then turn the form over.

4. To make your bear's nose, fold point G (front flap only) up, then back a little.

5. The last step is to tuck the back flap of point G inside the form, and your bear is done.

# A Super Seal

Create a seashore scene with this super seal at center stage.

**Directions**

1. Begin with Basic Form 4, with the open-ended flaps pointing to the left. Then use a mountain fold to fold the form in half, bringing point B to meet point A.

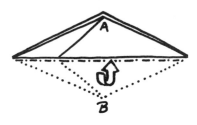

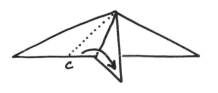

2. Fold point C back and down as shown in the illustration on both the front and back sides of the form, but don't turn the form over.

3. Next, fold and unfold both ends of the form to make the creases for the neck and tail.

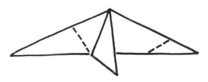

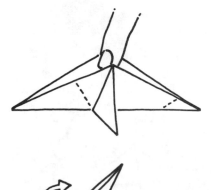

4. Take a moment to study the illustration. Now place your finger in the opening at the top of the form, then tuck the paper in at both folds to create the neck and the tail.

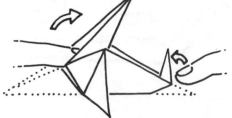

5. Making the head and snout is similar to step 4. This time fold and unfold the paper to make the creases as shown on the seal's neck.

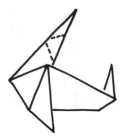

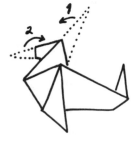

6. Tuck the paper in at crease 1 to make the head. Make the flattened snout by tucking in crease 2.

## One Step Further

**What You'll Need:**
shoebox lid • sand • pebbles • small rocks

To display your seal, fill a shoebox lid with sand and small pebbles. Give the seal a place to rest by adding a small, flat rock to your seashore scene.

# 31 ▷ Paper Pocket

If you use a large piece of paper, you can make an innovative envelope to hold all of those special deliveries your mail carrier brings.

**Directions**

1. Begin by using a valley fold to make a crease in the center of a square of paper. Next, fold sides 1 and 2 to meet at the crease.

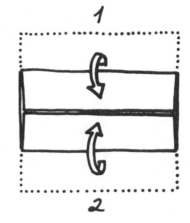

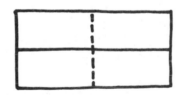

2. Using the valley fold again, fold and unfold to make a crease in the center. Then fold sides 3 and 4 to meet at the center line. Unfold your form again and you will have three sharp creases.

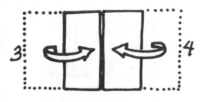

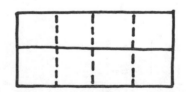

3. Now, fold down points A and B, fold in sides 3 and 4, then fold up points C and D to make a crease, then unfold them.

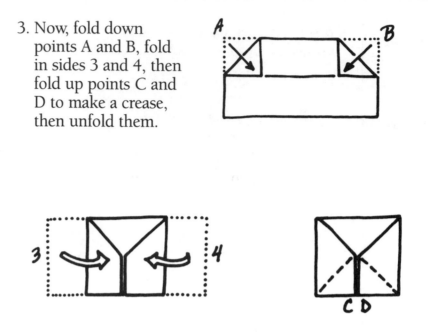

4. For the final step, use a valley fold to fold the form in half. Tuck points C and D into the triangular pockets in the upper half of the form and your paper pocket is complete.

# Star Quality

You'll twinkle with delight when you've completed this nifty star box for storing your favorite treasures.

## Directions

1. Begin your star box with Basic Form 6. Be sure the open end is up, then fold points A and B (front flaps only) to the center.

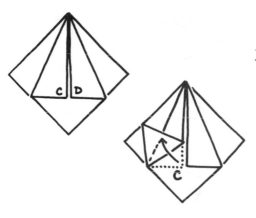

2. Firmly fold and unfold points C and D to make the creases as shown. Now lift the left "wing" of the triangle, open it slightly, and press down on point C to flatten it, then repeat this step with point D, turn the form over, and repeat this step on the other side.

3. Now you are ready to grasp point E (front flap only) and use a mountain fold to fold it back into the center. Repeat this step with point F, then turn the form over and repeat this step on the opposite side.

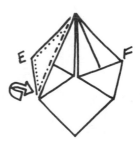

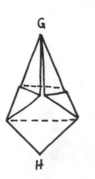

4. Using valley folds, fold and unfold points G and H to make sharp creases.

5. At the top of the form are four open points. To make the star box, take the shape, grasp the two outer points, and pull outward.

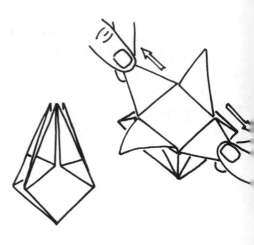

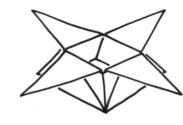

6. Flatten the base and your star box is complete.

**One Step Further**

This little box is an excellent way to present holiday candies. For a special New Year's treat, fill it with glitter or confetti to throw when the clock strikes midnight.

## Sly Fox

You'll look pretty sly when you show your friends how your pointy-eared fox appears to bark!

**Directions**

1. Begin by folding a square of paper in half as shown.

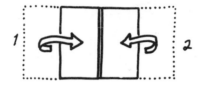

2. Next, fold sides 1 and 2 to the center line, then fold down points A and B.

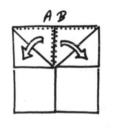

3. Now lift point A open. Push down to flatten it, then repeat this step with point B.

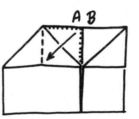

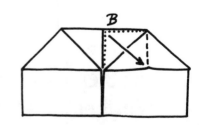

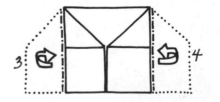

4. Use mountain folds to turn back sides 3 and 4.

5. Fold up point C (front flap only), then turn the form over and repeat this step on the opposite side.

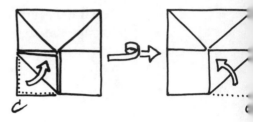

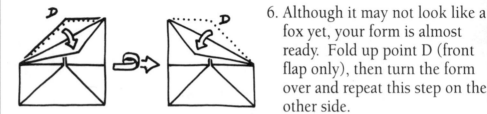

6. Although it may not look like a fox yet, your form is almost ready. Fold up point D (front flap only), then turn the form over and repeat this step on the other side.

7. Now slip your fingertips into the opening and pull the sides outward. Your fox will appear when you tuck in and close its mouth.

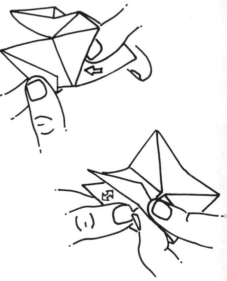

## One Step Further

**What You'll Need:**
scissors • glue • red felt

How about giving your clever fox a long red tongue? Cut a small piece of felt into the proper shape and glue it to the bottom of the animal's open mouth.

# Paper Pine Tree

You won't need water or soil to grow this paper pine tree, just your own nimble fingers. Why not fold a few and create a fabulous forest! You might pick a special one to write a holiday greeting on. Slip it in a paper pocket from page 59 and give it to a friend!

**Directions**

1. Begin each tree with Basic Form 4, then fold point A up as shown.

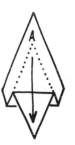

2. Now fold point A down again but not quite all the way.

3. One more time! Fold point A up about halfway and your first tree is complete. What could be easier?!

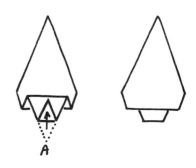

# Under the Big Top!

Use colorful paper to make this cheerful circus tent. A large square of gift-wrapping paper with stripes is perfect!

## Directions

1. Begin with your paper in a square. Fold sides 1 and 2 about half an inch in from the outside. If you're using a larger-than-average piece of paper, fold the sides in even more. Then use a valley fold to fold the form in half, bringing side 3 to meet side 4.

2. Now fold the form in half once more, this time bringing side 1 to meet side 2. Then unfold your form to make the crease as shown. You will need to make two more creases by folding and unfolding points E and F. If you make the creases sharp enough, the next step will be simple.

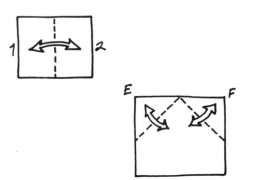

3. First, open the right side slightly. Then push down on point F and tuck the fold inside. Repeat this step with point E and your tent is ready to raise!

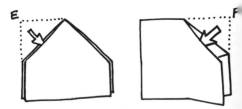

## One Step Further

**What You'll Need:**
sawdust • shoebox lid • toothpicks • colored paper • scissors • glue

Set the background for the "Greatest Show on Earth" by filling a shoebox lid with sawdust. Then cut tiny flags from colored paper and glue them to toothpicks. Use the flags to decorate your circus tent.

# Let's Make Music!

Here's a stand-up piano that will fit inside a notebook!

**Directions**

1. Begin with a square of paper and fold it in half from top to bottom, then fold the form in half once again, this time from side to side. Make a sharp crease, and unfold it.

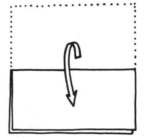

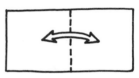

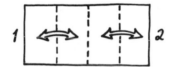

2. Carefully bring sides 1 and 2 into the center line. Make crisp, sharp creases and unfold them. Next, use the outer creases as a guide to fold points A and B down as shown.

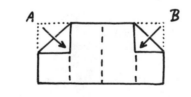

3. This next step can be challenging, but work slowly and you will get it. Lift the right side up at a right angle to the form and push down on point B to flatten it. Repeat this step with point A on the left side of the form.

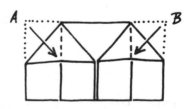

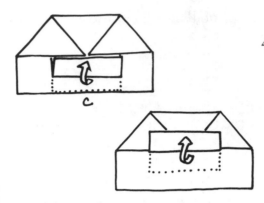

4. You are now ready to make the keyboard! Fold point C up so that it is level with the base of the triangles, then fold the same section of paper up one more tim

5. Now bring the sides in and the keyboard down and your stand-up piano is ready to play!

## One Step Further

**What You'll Need:**
fine-tipped marking pen • ruler

Add the finishing touch to your piano by neatly drawing in the keys. Make sure to use a ruler to make each line as straight as possible.

# Peter Paper Cottontail

You will need a pair of scissors to make this bouncing bunny's long ears spring to life.

## Directions

1. Begin with Basic Form 1 and fold point A toward point B, then back again about halfway.

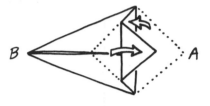

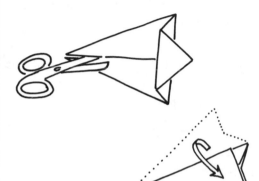

2. Do you have your scissors ready? Carefully make a cut like the one in the illustration. The length of the cut will be about one-third the size of your form, which you will then fold in half with a valley fold.

3. All that's left to do is to make the bunny's ears, and that's easily done by folding point B (front flap only) straight up. That's the first ear, and the second is made by doing the same thing to the back flap using a mountain fold.

## One Step Further

**What You'll Need:**
glue • cotton ball

Giving your bunny a fluffy tail is as easy as one, two, three. One—put a spot of glue on the rabbit's tail end. Two—form a cottontail to fit your bunny. Three—glue it in place to make a cottontail that really deserves its name!

# The Crowning Touch

It doesn't take long to make this royal headgear fit for a king or queen!

**Directions**

1. Begin with Basic Form 2 and fold points A and B up.

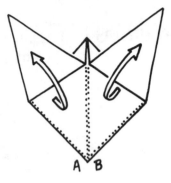

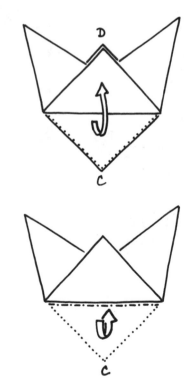

2. Now fold point C (front flap only) up to meet point D using a valley fold. Then use a mountain fold to fold the back flap at point C behind the form. Your crown is ready to wear!

**One Step Further**

**What You'll Need:**
glue • glitter • sequins

To make your coronation truly grand, decorate your crown with sequin gems and golden flecks of glitter. If you use a large piece of paper, you can perch your creation on your own head!

# 39 Beautiful Bird

This bird isn't very difficult to fold, but you will need scissors to make its lovely tail.

1. Begin with a square of paper and fold points A and B to the center, then use a valley fold to fold the form in half, bringing side 1 to meet side 2.

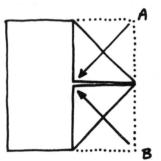

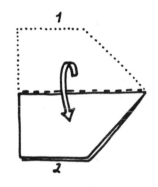

2. Next, make a sharp crease at point C, then tuck this point in to form the bird's head.

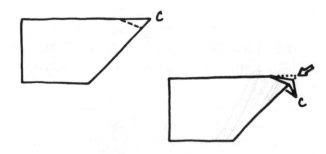

3. It's time to use your scissors. Carefully make a cut like the one in the illustration. The length of the cut will be slightly less that half the size of the form.

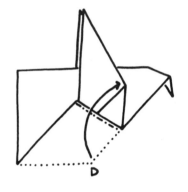

4. Once your cut is finished, use a valley fold to fold point D (front flap only) straight up. Do the same with the back flap, using a mountain fold, and your bird is ready for flight.

## One Step Further

### What You'll Need:

glue • feathers • scissors • glitter

Make your bird very special by gluing feathers to its wings and flowing tail. Place two drops of glue where its eyes should be and sprinkle on little glitter to give this beautiful bird a sparkling gaze.

# Rock-a-Bye Baby

This little baby comes wrapped in its own blanket.

**Directions**

1. Begin with Basic Form 1 and use a mountain fold to fold back point A.

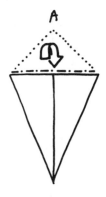

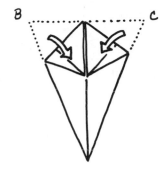

2. Next, fold points B and C to the center and turn your form over.

3. This part is a little tricky, so go slowly. Lift the upper square, reach inside, and fold points E and F to the center.

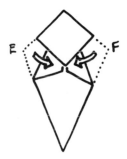

4. To complete your baby, fold back points G, H, and I, and get ready to sing a lullaby!

**One Step Further**

**What You'll Need:**
fine-tipped marker • yarn • ribbon

First, draw a face on your baby, then give it a few curls of yarn hair. If it is a little girl you may want to add a ribbon.

# Here Comes Santa Claus!

It only takes a few simple folds to make this jolly fellow!

**Directions**

1. Start with Basic Form 1. Be sure the open side is down and toward the back. Carefully fold points A and B to the center line and use a valley fold to fold the form in half. You will have a triangle with the open point at the top.

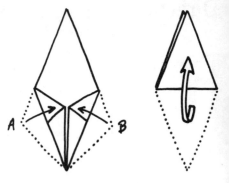

2. Fold the flaps at point C down so that the points just touch side 1.

3. You're almost finished. Make Santa's pointed hat by lifting point C (this time the front flap only) and folding it back—but not quite all the way. Fold back both sides using mountain folds and Santa will appear.

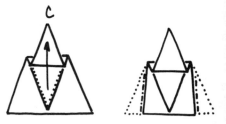

**One Step Further**

**What You'll Need:**
cotton ball • glue • fine-tipped marker

Draw in Santa's face and glue on a cotton wool beard. You might want to add a little cotton trim around his hat and a pom-pom at the very top. Ho ho ho!

# Sitting Pretty Puppy

This is a two-part form. To make this pleasant puppy you will need to add the form for Precious Pup on page 42. When it is complete, this puppy will always sit when it's told.

## Directions

1. Make your puppy's body by folding a square of paper in half to form a triangle.

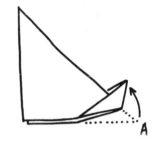

2. To make its wagging tail, fold back point A as shown in the illustration.

3. Now slip Precious Pup's head onto its body. Wasn't that simple?!

# Fun Flowers

Even in the middle of winter you can have a bounty of spring flowers. Why not fold a bouquet of tulips from several sheets of paper in a rainbow of colors? You might give each flower a stem by looking at page 77.

**Directions**

1. Begin with a square of paper turned to form a diamond shape. Fold the paper in half and then fold over point A to meet point B. Then carefully repeat this step with the left side of the triangle, bringing point C to meet point D.

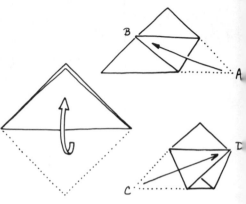

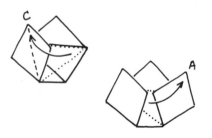

2. This is a little tricky. Lift point C up at a right angle to the form. Got that? Now push down on point C to flatten the form. Repeat this step with point A. It's easier now that you've had practice.

3. Use a mountain fold to fold back sides 1 and 2, then use a mountain fold again, but this time fold the entire form in half.

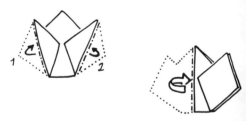

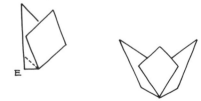

4. Fold up point E. Be sure to make a sharp crease, then unfold it. Now if you open the petals slightly and tuck in the base, your first flower is complete.

# A Place for Your Posies

The origami tulip on page 76 or any origami flower will look even
prettier at the tip of this stem with one slender leaf.

## Directions

1. Begin with Basic Form 1, turning
   the open end down. Neatly fold
   points A and B to the center,
   then turn the form over and use
   a valley fold to fold it in half,
   bringing point C to meet point D.

2. Use a valley fold to fold the form
   in half again, but this time bring
   point E to meet point F.

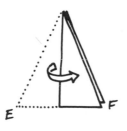

3. To complete the stem, crease the
   form as shown in the illustration.
   Then, as if you're peeling a
   banana, pull back on point C
   (back flap only) to make a
   delicate curved leaf.

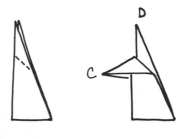

# Funny Frog

With the help of a pair of scissors you can make this frog look real enough to hop into your heart!

**Directions**

1. Begin with Basic Form 4 (open end down), then use a mountain fold to bring point A back to meet point B.

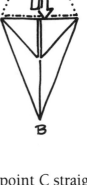

2. Next, lift point C straight up and flatten the right side of the form, then repeat this step with the left side of the form.

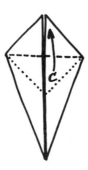

3. You've almost completed the frog's body. Fold points D and E in to the center line.

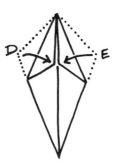

4. Using a valley fold, fold point B (front flap only) up. Then use your scissors to cut the remaining back flap from point B to a little beyond the center.

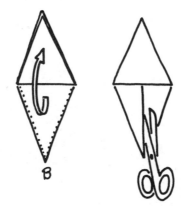

5. Next, turn your form over and carefully fold points F and G to the center.

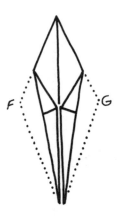

6. Are you ready to make the frog's arms and legs? Simply fold out each point as shown in the illustration.

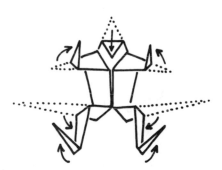

7. The head and feet are easy to make by using the illustration to guide you as you fold. Now turn your form over and *voilà*, you have a frog!

RIBBET!

# A Clever Crustacean

You will need a pair of scissors to make this little crab.

**Directions**

1. Begin with Basic Form 8, then use a valley fold to fold down side 1 to meet the center line.

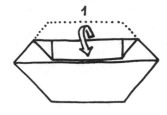

2. Next, take out your scissors and make four small cuts in the upper flap as shown in the illustration.

3. Now fold up the cuts to form the crab's eyes. Then fold up points A and B to form the base of the body.

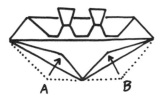

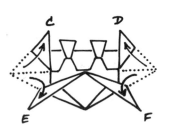

4. The legs and claws are last. Make them by folding points C, D, E, and F as shown in the illustration, then turn the form over and your crab is ready to crawl.

# Plucky Paper Penguin

You can use any color of paper to make your plucky paper penguin, but to make this Antarctic bird more realistic, use black paper with a white underside and your penguin will have its proper tuxedo!

## Directions

1. Begin with Basic Form 1. Use a mountain fold to fold the form in half, then fold back point A, but not quite all the way. Use the illustration as a guide. Turn the form over and repeat this step.

2. Now fold point A down again as shown. Turn the form over and repeat this on the other side.

3. To make the penguin's head, fold and crease the form as shown, then tuck in the fold.

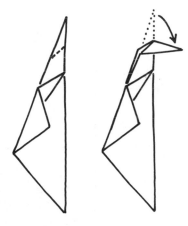

4. The penguin will stand if you make a crease at the bottom of the form as shown, then tuck the paper inside the form. Brrrrrrrr . . . your Antarctic bird is complete.

# Holiday Basket

On Valentine's Day use red paper to make this charming basket and fill it with candy hearts for someone special. On Easter fill it with little candy eggs!

**Directions**

1. Begin with a square of paper. Use a valley fold to fold side 1 to meet side 2 so that the open end is at the top. Make a half-inch fold along one side (or greater than a half-inch if your paper is larger than usual). Crease the paper, then cut along the crease and put aside the extra piece until later.

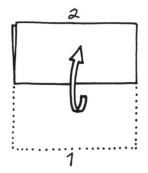

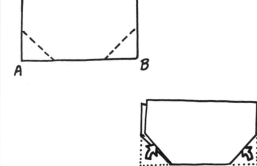

2. Fold points A and B up and back to make the creases as shown, then tuck points A and B inside the form.

3. Using valley folds, fold sides 3 and 4 (front flap only) so that they meet at the center line. Now use mountain folds to repeat this step with the back flap.

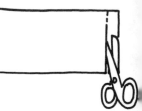

4. Now it's time to use that extra piece of paper you set aside. Make the basket's handle by folding both sides lengthwise into the center.

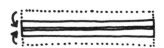

5. Slip one end into the form as shown in the illustration. Next, fold side 5 (front flap only) down twice so that the second fold is tucked into the basket.

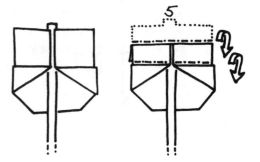

6. Here's where it gets a little tricky. Turn the basket over, lift the handle up and over, and loop it into the open flaps in the middle of the form, then repeat step 5 on this side.

7. Finally, make a sharp crease across the bottom of the form, then open the basket and flatten it at the base.

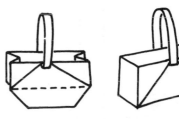

# Jungle Cat

This jungle cat will be happy to sit beside you whenever you want company.  Use any color paper you like, but be sure to draw on a cute face to make your cat complete.  You might give it spots to make it a leopard, or turn it into a tiger with real tiger stripes!

**Directions**

1. Begin with Basic Form 1 (open end down), then use a valley fold to bring point A to meet point B.

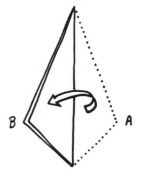

2. Fold down point C about half-way as shown in the illustration. Crease the paper sharply, then unfold it.

3. Study the drawing before you begin this next step.  Now use a valley fold to fold back side 1 (front flap only) toward side 2 so that your paper is shaped like that in the illustration.  The top of your form will curve slightly. When this is accomplished, fold down point C again.

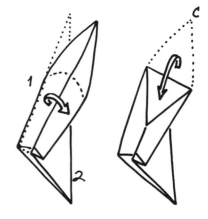

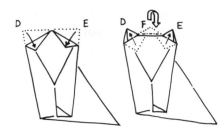

4. It's time to make the kitty's ears. First, use valley folds to fold down points D and E. Next, use a mountain fold to turn back point F. Finally, fold back points D and E again.

5. The kitty's face is a little tricky so, once again, study the illustration carefully before you begin. Find the crease at the center of the face. Place one finger a little to the left of the crease. With your other finger on the right side of the crease, push the paper to the left and flatten it as shown in the illustration. Got that? Now use a mountain fold to tuck point C under the kitty's face.

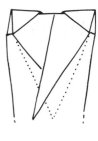

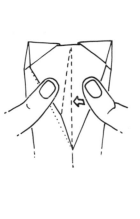

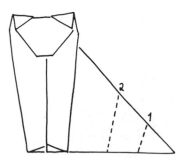

6. To make the tail, fold and unfold point G, making two sharp creases as shown. Now open the form slightly and tuck crease 1 into crease 2.

7. The final detail is to fold back sides 1 and 2 to create the kitty's slender front legs. Grrrrrrrrrrr!

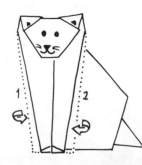

When is a hat not a hat? When it's a fish! You'll see for yourself when you use a pair of scissors to turn Hatful of Fun on page 23 into this adorable angelfish.

**Directions**

1. Begin by following the steps to make the Hatful of Fun, but when you get to step 3, don't fold in the back flap.

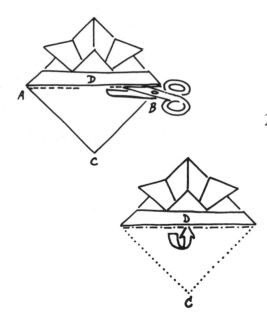

2. Use your scissors to make a cut on each side of the back flap at points A and B. Each cut should be about two-thirds of the way to the center. When you are finished with this step, use a mountain fold to fold back point C.

3. Now hold the hat at point D and turn the form to the side. Grip point C (single flap only) at the back of the form and gently pull both points in opposite directions to see your fish take shape.

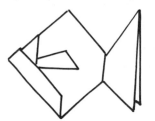

4. Last but not least, flatten the form and your finny friend is ready to swim.

# Origami Gets Even More Original!

There are so many different things you can do with origami, it's truly amazing! In this chapter, you'll find all sorts of ideas and uses for the origami crafts you've created—from decorating the house for a special holiday to brightening up a corner of your room. (And wait till you see the ideas on hosting your own origami party!)

## Fun and Functional

Not only is origami beautiful to look at, but you can also construct some origami pieces to be used around the house or in your room.

If you have a penchant for pictures but can't afford expensive frames, make the The Great Frame Fold-Up! on page 28. You can even fold your own jewelry, such as the adorable Friendship Ring on page 52. Increase the life span of your ring by coating it with clear varnish or rubber cement.

The Cute Cup and Handy Holder (pages 46 and 47) will both prove very useful if you ever need containers for those precious "valuables," like jelly beans, pennies, or cool rocks!

## Handmade Holiday Cheer

Holidays are the perfect time to create stunning handmade origami decorations for your walls and tables. Following you'll find some great ideas for bringing out the origami spirit all year long!

**New Year's Eve:** Create unique confetti containers on page 61 with Star Quality. To further decorate your stars use colorful markers to write in the new year that you and your friends are celebrating.

**Valentine's Day:** Fold a decorative gift box for that special friend, then fill it with his or her favorite candied hearts. Wrap It Up, the gift box found on page 36, can be created with red or pink paper. Or find some special Valentine's Day wrapping paper and cut it down to the size you want for your box.

Fold up the Paper Pocket on pages 59 and 60 to hold an extra-secret Valentine's message. Depending on what size of paper you use, you can make a large envelope or a small, precious one. Seal it closed with your favorite Valentine's stickers. (A piece of clear tape works, too.)

**Easter:** No Easter holiday is complete without the treasured Easter basket. Make your own mini-baskets (A Tisket, a Tasket on page 27), then fill them with green tissue paper and jelly beans. They're so easy, you can make one for each member of your family.

**Halloween:** Turn the Hot-Air Balloon on page 48 into a frightening jack-o'-lantern! Just follow the directions for the Hot-Air Balloon, using bright orange origami paper. With a black marker, fill in gruesome or goofy facial features, your choice. Then top off your pumpkin with a piece of green pipe cleaner for its stem!

**Christmas:** Fill your house with the spirit of this winter holiday—the decorations are easy to make and look great! Try the Paper Pine Tree on page 65, then decorate it with colorful sequins and rhinestones. Create a chorus of beautiful angels (found on page 25). You may even want to attach thin lengths of fishing line to their halos and hang them from the ceiling for an angelic ensemble.

**Hanukkah:** Create beautiful candles and candle holders to decorate the holiday dinner table or your bedroom. Simply fold a pair of Creative Candle Cradles (page 33) using silver or white origami paper. Next fold a pair of Clever Candles (page 35) with bright blue paper. These attractive candles and holders will complement the joyous Festival of Lights.

**Room with a View**

Everyone knows about painting walls or hanging wallpaper to decorate a room. But you can have a look that's all your own—your friends will beg you to show them how you did it—when you use your imagination and get down to some serious decorating with origami!

The wonderful thing about using origami figures for making your room more attractive is that you can switch colors, add to them, or take them down easily when you want a change of scenery. Here are some ideas to get you thinking:

## Pleasing Presents

Origami is not only perfect for decorating rooms and livening up parties, so check out these fun origami projects that are ideal for gift-giving!

- Fun Flowers (page 76) displayed in a cute vase, A Place for Your Posies (page 77)

- Friendship Ring (page 52)—created using your and your friend's favorite colors!

**Pet-in-a-Bowl**: Here are some pets you never have to feed! Create a few turtles (page 55) or frogs (page 78) using different green-colored paper. Find an old empty fishbowl (a glass bowl will work, too) and cover the bottom with sand, pretty rocks, or dried twigs. Stick your pets in the bowl to create a fun pond scene without the trouble of water!

**I Love Cats and Dogs Mobile**: To create the base for your mobile, simply take two long sticks or dowels and cross them in the middle. Secure them together with strong string or cord. Now choose your pets. You may want to pick the cute dog and cat head shapes, Precious Pup/Cuddly Kitty, found on page 42, or fold the full bodies of the pets. Sitting Pretty Puppy is found on page 75, and Jungle Cat is on page 84. Fold your origami and decorate as you wish. Then take a thin piece of string and attach it to the top of each animal shape. Tie the other end of each string to the mobile. Have an adult help you hang the mobile from the ceiling. Are the puppies chasing the kitties, or is it the other way around?

**A Bounty of Birds**: For this mobile you'll need a large branch with smaller branches and twigs. Choose five to eight origami birds and fold them, using the brightest origami paper you have. A variety of flying creatures can be found throughout, such as Chattering Bird (page 41), Fluttering Butterfly (page 54), and Beautiful Bird (pages 71 and 72). You may even want to add some pesky flies (page 43)! Hang a couple from the branches and stick a few among the twigs. Ask an adult to help you hang the finished craft from the ceiling.

**A Day at Sea**: For the nautical lover in you, fill a blank wall with an entire ocean scene. (For this project you'll need to tape or thumbtack poster board to the wall. Check with your parents for an okay first.)

To create the backdrop, you'll need both a light blue piece of poster board and a darker blue piece. Depending on how much space you have, fit the two pieces so that the light blue is on the top half for the sky and the dark blue board is just below the lighter board, representing the ocean.

Now it's your turn to get creative! Make a bright red sailboat (page 22) on the top of the ocean or a crab crawling along the ocean floor (page 80). Create a variety of colorful fish (page 86). You may even want to glue some silver sequins on them to give the illusion of shiny scales. Use the directions to make the Hot-Air Balloon (page 48) to create a bright yellow sun hanging high in the sky. Add a seal (page 57) playing in the water with a gigantic whale (page 40). In this ocean environment anything goes! Once you've created all your origami pieces, you'll want to attach fishing line to the top of each one to hang from the ceiling. Cut the lengths of line so that the boat appears to float along the top of the water, the fish look like they're swimming in the ocean, and the crab is on the floor of the ocean.

Your Day at Sea will be in constant motion as the origami pieces catch the slightest breezes and bounce and move along the waves!

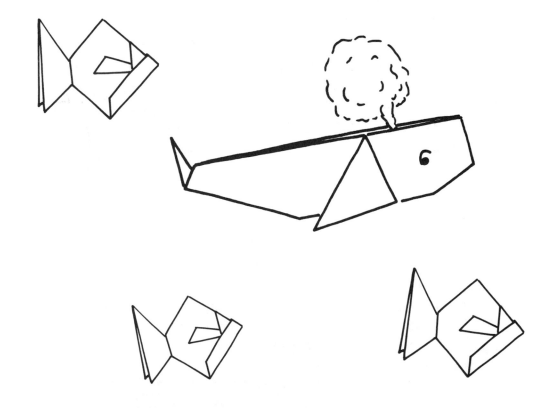

## The Ultimate Origami-Rama!

Imagine a party that's totally different than any you've ever been to—an origami original! Personalize party goods by using origami for invitations, place cards, decorations, favor bags, and art projects.

Start off your party plans by making an origami invitation for each guest. Pick any origami object you like that has enough space to write the time, place, and date of your party. Or, if your friends are as crazy about origami as you are, send an unfolded sheet of origami paper with the party details. Then have each person create his or her own origami craft from the enclosed paper and bring it to the party to share. Display the origami on a bookshelf or table for all to admire.

When it comes to decorating for your party, try one of these incredible centerpieces to adorn the food and drink table or any other space you wish:

### Top It Off!

Origami crafts are perfect for decorating packages. Here are some ideas to beautify and personalize your gifts:

- Rock-a-Bye Baby (page 73)—looks adorable on baby shower gifts!

- Here Comes Santa Claus! (page 74)—add your own cheerful face to this Santa head

- Let's Make Music! (page 67)—for your favorite music lover, his or her very own piano

- Fun Flowers (page 76)—always appropriate on any gift for Mom, Grandma, or that special aunt

**The Ocean**: Cover your table with sheets of crinkled blue tissue paper. The crinkles will give the paper an ocean wave look. Then create a Finny Friend (page 86) for each guest. Spread the cute fish around the table and invite your friends to take one home after the evening is over. On page 40 you can find out how to create a gigantic whale in A Whale of an Idea. Don't forget to stick some cotton in the large whale's spout to suggest spurting water! If you have room, create a few Super Simple Sailboats (page 22) in bright colors to complement the blue water.

**In the Country**: Create an outdoor centerpiece that's a sweet barnyard scene. First, sprinkle the table with hay on which you can set your origami pieces. Choose your favorite animals from this book to fill the yard, such as a pig (page 18), a hen (page 38), butterflies (page 54), a rabbit (page 69), and a couple of frogs (page 78). Don't forget to "build" a big bright red barn, too, found on page 20.

If you have time, you may want to fold up little party favors for each friend, like a beautiful basket filled with candy (page 82), a friendship ring (page 52), or a pinwheel that really spins (page 31).

At your party, supply a variety of colorful paper so all your guests can join in the paper-folding fun. Be sure to have on hand glue, glitter, and anything else that can be used to decorate your paper crafts. This will be one party that's unforgettable!

## For More Information

If you just can't get enough on origami, the Friends of the Origami Center of America would love to hear from you. They are a nonprofit organization whose mission is to spread knowledge of origami as an art and a craft.

They have groups across the country, and you can find out more information about them by sending a self-addressed, stamped envelope with two first-class stamps to:

Friends of the Origami Center of America
15 West 77th Street
New York, NY 10024

They also have a Website! Check it out at: www.origami-usa.org

# Look for these other
# 50 Nifty **SUPER** titles:

50 Nifty SUPER Friendship Crafts

50 Nifty SUPER Magic Tricks

50 Nifty SUPER Scary Crafts and Other Things to Do

50 Nifty SUPER Science Experiments

50 Nifty SUPER Science Fair Projects